Exploring Worship in Pilgrimage

Helen Bent
Head of Ministerial Training,
Royal School of Church Music in Partnership with Praxis
and Associate Priest, Walgrave Benefice,
Diocese of Peterborough

GROVE BOOKS LIMITED
RIDLEY HALL RD CAMBRIDGE CB3 9HU

Contents

Acknowledgments

This booklet has been written during the Coronavirus lockdown, when travel anywhere has been impossible. Many of the 2020 Year of Pilgrimage celebrations and events have been cancelled or postponed. It therefore feels all the more important to recognize the significance of special places and the value of journey at this time when both are being denied to us. As so often, we discover what we most value when it is taken away from us.

I would like to thank members of the Group for Renewal of Worship who have supported me in the writing of this booklet. I am grateful for their friendship. Particular thanks are due to Mark Earey and Anne Harrison who helped to hone the text with their sharp critique and suggestions.

Liturgical texts published by the Royal School of Church Music (www.rscm.org.uk) and the Iona Community (www.ionabooks.com) are used with permission.

First Impression August 2020
ISSN 0144-1728
ISBN 978 1 78827 134 9

Introduction

1

This booklet has been inspired by a growing fascination with pilgrimage during the 21st century and by the 2020 Year of Pilgrimage, organized by the Association of English Cathedrals, which corresponds with multiple commemorations and with the reopening of various long-distance pilgrim walks.[1] Pilgrimage appeals to people of different faiths and none, borne out by several recent television series exploring significant spiritual routes.

Although there are already two booklets on pilgrimage in the Grove Spirituality series, *Pilgrimage* by David Osborne (S59) and *Pilgrimage Today* by Peter Gibbs (S143), this booklet has been written with worship as the primary focus.[2] It is intended for both would-be pilgrims who want to add a more intentional worship dynamic into their pilgrimage, and for worship leaders who want to facilitate such worship. It is also for those who want to make their churches into accessible and inviting worship spaces for visitors and enquirers outside normal service times, rather than mere places of architectural and historical interest. Pilgrimage gives us a wonderful opportunity to connect with the worshipping church—past, present and future.

My own interest in this subject has grown ever since walking the 62.5 miles of St Cuthbert's Way from Melrose in the Scottish Borders to Holy Island off the Northumbrian coast. What began as a long-distance walk with friends was unexpectedly transformed into a pilgrimage. *En route* to Melrose, we visited St Cuthbert's tomb in Durham Cathedral. There we lit candles and prayed; our pilgrimage had begun. From then on, this became not only a walk together but also a walk with God, punctuated by theological conversations and opportunities to draw aside for prayer and contemplation, alone and together. The journey was full of special moments, but praying in Cuthbert's cave was particularly poignant. We experienced a range of typical British weather, culminating in the barefoot walk across the sands to Lindisfarne in a howling gale and driving rain. Head down, battling the elements, there was a very real connection with the pilgrims of earlier centuries and their commitment to proclaim the gospel. After visiting the Priory and the Lindisfarne Gospels, we completed our day with Evening Prayer in St Mary's Church, a fitting end to my first act of pilgrimage. After that I was hooked!

My fascination has continued, developing a more deliberate liturgical expression. The theme of Christian pilgrimage ran through the RSCM International

Summer School in August 2019, as we explored the cell of Mother Julian in Norwich, the Shrine of Our Lady at Walsingham, and some of the most spectacular angel roofs of East Anglia. Here, worship was explicitly linked with the places visited through their liturgy and music. Most recently, I spent some time exploring the vast numbers of Celtic crosses and Celtic-Norse keeills (chapels) on the Isle of Man. Here again, with the reopening of two long-distance footpaths in 2020, there are opportunities to delve into the worship history of the island. There is a rich blend of Manx, Celtic and contemporary spirituality, fertile soil again for developing worship elements within an act of pilgrimage.

To review this ancient tradition, and reinterpret it for a twenty-first century church, it may be useful to establish a working definition of pilgrimage. A pilgrimage involves a long journey or search, important to a person's beliefs and faith, usually taking a long time over a great distance toward a specific destination of significance. Two key elements are held in tension: journey—this has more significance than just getting from A to B—and place. Both starting point and destination may hold special significance.

The word has its roots in the Latin *peregrinus* which suggests roving, wandering or migration; a journey generally made on foot. It might involve a route to a sacred place to show respect, or a spiritual quest for some exalted purpose or moral significance, perhaps an act of penance or thanksgiving. In its general sense, a pilgrimage could equally be a secular journey made for sentimental reasons: to explore family roots or to return to a much-loved place of significance, linked to a rite of passage, for example. We engage with the surroundings, the history and other people on the way.

Motivation may vary, but pilgrimage blends the physical, mental, emotional and spiritual into one unified experience. The traveller, or pilgrim, intentionally withdraws from the usual daily environment, and the journey itself can be of as much value as the final destination. David Osborne states, 'This journey is being undertaken for some purpose beyond entertainment that has something to do with the person's identity and life story.'[3] There is an introspective aspect here where pilgrims connect with self, especially when set apart from a busy world. Resonance is found with the twenty-first century quest for experience, but these desires may hide a deeper hunger and a spiritual vacuum in the lives of many. Some who set out on pilgrimage are searchers looking for meaning. The process of journey allows ambiguity and conflicting emotions to be held in tension and creates the space to process these feelings at a deeper level and in a safe space.

2

Worship's Role in Pilgrimage

Pilgrimage has been described as an ancient tradition in tune with today's needs, providing an opportunity to step aside from the busyness of our lives. Although its origins are difficult to determine, pilgrimage is a common feature in many world religions. Jews might journey to Jerusalem for festivals, and Muslims might journey to Mecca at least once in their lifetime as their ultimate act of worship. However, there are constant tensions within Christianity between the veneration of place and the realization that place cannot determine our ability to connect with God; between religious tourism and genuine devotion; between the need to escape from life and an urgency for faith to connect with everyday life more incisively.

Biblical Background—An Inherent Tension

Initially, Old Testament worship was on the hoof during journeys of necessity with a pattern of building altars to enable worship on the way. After the exodus from Egypt, the tabernacle provided a focus to prevent the Israelites straying from the worship of the one true God, but the tabernacle was not dependent on place as such; it travelled with them from place to place. When King David took the ark of the Lord to Jerusalem, only then was the city established as the centre of Jewish worship (2 Sam 6.12ff). This was consolidated by the building of the temple, which became a place of pilgrimage for subsequent generations.

In the New Testament, we frequently find Jesus at the temple for one of the Jewish festivals, but during his conversation with the woman at the well, he challenges the idea of worshipping in a specific place. The Samaritans had worshipped on Mount Gerizim, the Jews in Jerusalem, but Jesus tells the woman, 'True worshippers will worship the Father in spirit and truth, for they are the kind of worshippers the Father seeks' (John 4.23). The significance of place is surpassed by the importance of the attitude of the worshippers and their relationship with God. Like Jesus, Paul showed little interest in place. He worshipped anywhere and everywhere, whenever opportunity arose. In Paul's terms, believers themselves become temples of the Holy Spirit, carrying God's presence within (1 Cor 6.19).

Pilgrimage to the Holy Land

Pilgrimage frequently combines individual spirituality and corporate worship. My own approach began from a worship perspective; an interest in pilgrimage came later. However, within antiquity, pilgrimage comes first and worship follows. Further stimulus for the development of pilgrimage came from Constantine's mother Helena, who popularized the idea of visiting places associated with the life of Christ. Churches were built at important biblical sites for celebrating the events connected with them, enabling pilgrims to relive sacred history *in situ*. The pilgrim could visualize the biblical narrative better, even if the streets were not the exact same streets that Jesus walked. This arrival of pilgrims stimulated a development of liturgy, pioneering much of the annual cycle of seasonal worship we experience today.

We owe much of our liturgical information to a remarkable fourth-century pilgrim, Egeria.[4] At a crucial stage of liturgical development, her writings put worship at the heart of her pilgrimage experience. Her detailed accounts describe a fully developed daily office and a clear sense of journeying through the church year. Egeria draws particular attention to Holy Week and embryonic Stations of the Cross, which we will explore later.

Celtic Saints

Celtic saints set out on pilgrimage for different reasons. Here we find a strong sense of calling and missionary zeal. According to tradition, Patrick, the fifth century 'apostle to Ireland,' fasted and prayed for forty days on Croagh Patrick, a mountain in County Mayo. Present-day pilgrims still climb to the oratory, sometimes barefoot, carrying a stone to add to the cairn at the top as an act of penance or a prayer intention. Some Celtic saints chose white martyrdom, setting out by land or sea with no specific destination in mind, reliant on the wind of the Spirit to guide them. Following Paul's example on his missionary journeys, Brendan, Columba and Aidan walked long distances, evangelizing on their way. They established monasteries for the sake of mission, but place was secondary. Nevertheless, present-day pilgrims now follow in their footsteps, travelling to Lindisfarne or Iona to immerse themselves in the regular rhythms of daily worship with a desire to grow in holiness.

The Growth of Significant Pilgrim Routes

According to Pope Benedict XVI, other than the Holy Land, 'Pilgrims go to Rome, the city of the martyrdom of Peter and Paul, and also Compostela, which, associated with the memory of St James, has welcomed pilgrims throughout the world who desire to strengthen their spirit with the apostle's witness of faith and love.'[5] Although Santiago de Compostela was founded as a focus of pilgrimage during the Middle Ages, there has been a huge resurgence of pilgrimage there during the twenty-first century, attracting people from around the world. Deeply embedded within the journey is the knowledge that thousands of people have done this before. For many, moments of contemplation give a sense of heritage, peace and devotion. Whilst French churches are often open, Spanish churches are more often closed, affording limited worship opportunities *en route*. Thus, the pilgrim mass at Santiago cathedral is seen as the climax.

The twelfth century is largely regarded as the golden age of Christian pilgrimage. Smaller and more local pilgrimage sites also enjoyed great popularity, usually associated with the burial of local saints or martyrs such as Etheldreda at Ely, Chad at Lichfield and Thomas Becket in Canterbury. This was seen as a way of invoking the help of a saint for desperate people suffering from disease or terrified of hell. The journey was an act of penance which culminated in a mass in the hope of taking time off purgatory. Big business in the Middle Ages, this lucrative racket preyed on this ignorance and fear.

Protestant Reaction

Unsurprisingly, the Reformers were unanimous in their condemnation, reacting against indulgences and relics and the exploitation of the ignorant or gullible for financial gain. In their eyes, pilgrimage promoted superstition and idolatry rather than true faith. God's grace was not received by long arduous journeys or bought with money. In 1538, Henry VIII and Thomas Cromwell banned pilgrimage in Britain and the tradition lay fallow.

There is no mention of pilgrimage in *The Book of Common Prayer*, but the motif of journey recurs in art and literature. John Bunyan's *The Pilgrim's Progress* (1678–1684) is widely regarded as one of the most influential works of English literature and Puritan faith. However, Bunyan expands the pilgrimage idea to make it an allegory of life rather than an actual journey. Still the idea of pilgrimage persists, taking on new forms. Camp meetings in the American west during the nineteenth century attracted great crowds gathering from unchurched settlements in search of worship and spiritual nourishment, the forerunners of annual gatherings like Greenbelt, Spring Harvest and New Wine.

Contemporary Expressions

Contemporary expressions include pilgrimages to both Protestant and Catholic sites. Some walk ancient pilgrim paths to English cathedrals; many visit sites associated with apparitions of the Virgin Mary, such as Walsingham, Lourdes and Fatima. The communities of Iona and Taizé welcome thousands of pilgrims of various denominations each year. Present-day pilgrims are also drawn together to remember Christian martyrs. In Zimbabwe and Uganda, large annual pilgrimages to places of martyrdom are accompanied by great commemorations, full of colour and energy.[6]

During the twenty-first century, we have seen the inclusion of multi-sensory elements within worship in the form of labyrinths and prayer stations. We could argue that the journey is significant for labyrinth experiences. Despite not travelling anywhere, we move into the centre towards God and then outwards back into the world. Indeed, there are suggestions that this could be an alternative for those unable to travel to Jerusalem.[7] By contrast, with prayer stations destination is all important. Here we can vary the order, linger at particular stations or miss out others that do not appeal. Pilgrimage holds both journey and destination together.

Alongside contemporary expressions of pilgrimage, the question of so-called 'thin' places has arisen, adopted from George MacLeod, founder of the Iona community. MacLeod described Iona as a 'thin place—only a tissue paper separating earth from heaven,' suggesting that the veil between this world and the eternal world, between spirit and matter, is thinner at certain locations than others.[8] Although physicality is important to human beings, God is not more present in some places than others. This brings us full circle to where we began with the inherent tensions between journey and place. That does not mean there are not places or ways of doing things that we may find spiritually more uplifting than others. The nub of the matter is perhaps summed up in an ancient Celtic saying: 'To go to Rome is much trouble, little profit. The king whom you seek there you will not find, unless you take him with you.'[9]

Questions for Reflection

- When does a walk become transformed into an authentic act of pilgrimage?
- How do we differentiate between religious tourism, retreat and pilgrimage?
- When and where does a pilgrimage begin and end?
- In a culture of pick-and-mix spirituality, what is unique about Christian pilgrimage?
- How might worship 'on the way' be encouraged?

Exploring Pilgrim Liturgies

3

This chapter explores two sorts of worship, drawing on the pilgrimage ideas outlined in chapter two:

- Acts of worship, which are part of an actual pilgrimage;
- Static services, which draw on the theme of pilgrimage or journey.

The second type of service reminds us that in the early church, the Christian life was referred to as 'The Way' and Christians were known as 'people of the way' (Acts 9.2). Pilgrimage was therefore a core metaphor for understanding the Christian life as well as a physical activity in which to participate.

Ancient Liturgies and the Significance of Story

The three great Jewish festivals not only involved a physical journey up to Jerusalem, but also the active remembering of previous epic journeys: the great exodus from Egypt (Passover); the long walk to Mount Sinai (Shavuot or Feast of Tabernacles); and the years spent wandering in the wilderness (Sukkot or Feast of Weeks). As these events were celebrated, the present generation was drawn into the metanarrative of God's dealing with his people through a process of conscious engagement.

The Passover meal could not begin until questions about its significance had been asked, usually by the youngest child of the household, answered by the father.

Why do we eat unleavened bread?
Why do we eat bitter herbs?
Why do we dip our food in liquid?
Why do we eat in a reclining position?

The directness demands explanation, our curiosity is aroused and we are drawn in to hear more. This principle is adopted in one of the *Common Worship* Additional Eucharistic Prayers for use with children. The questions help the whole congregation to engage more fully with what is being said. Why not use a similar principle to invite the congregation into pilgrim worship? Sample questions might be:

Question: Why have pilgrims walked this path?
Answer: Follow, and together we will see.
Question: Why have pilgrims worshipped here?
Answer: Follow, and together we will hear.
Question: How do we follow the way of Christ today?
Answer: Follow, and together we will learn.

The ancient Jewish festivals are also imbued with a sense of dislocation, journey and homecoming. Kathy Galloway explores this in *The Pattern of our Days*. She offers four exodus liturgies entitled Home, Exile, Desert, Promised Land. The worship journey enables reflection on the conflicting emotions of wilderness experiences as well as a longing for the promised land and a place to settle. These liturgies could provide a powerful framework to help congregations return to church after time out, after a crisis or after a reordering. The liturgies could be used on separate occasions, or all four sections together could form the basis of an 'unlock' service or 'celebration full of renewal and hope.' Indeed, the first three sections could happen at significant points outside, reflecting on essentials we valued before (home), the loss and deprivation of absence (exile), lessons learnt by experience (desert) and moving back inside to embrace the new normal (promised land).

Each section begins with a call to worship:

The people gather facing one another. Short responses between right and left side of the congregation follow:

Leader The Lord says: When the time comes,
I will answer the prayers of my people.
Left The Lord will say: You are my people.
Right We will answer: You are our God.
Left Once you had not received mercy.
Right Now you have received mercy.
All **This is our hope, our living hope.**
We shall be glad.

Leader The Lord says: When the time comes,
I will lead you as a shepherd to fresh pastures.[10]

The repetition of these opening responses is powerful, building to a crescendo in the final homecoming section. The leader's final line changes as the service progresses, reminding us that God remains with us even in exile, woos us in the wilderness, and restores us with gladness and joy. A solidarity with the past renews confidence in God in the present. For example, after a period of online services or complete worship deprivation during the Coronavirus pandemic, we are a changed people, shaped by the experiences of the previous months. As travellers, we often hold ambiguity and conflicting emotions within ourselves, but pilgrimage allows personal story to be shared with casual conversation often moving quickly to honest reflection and disclosure. Opportunities for sharing in small groups or including testimony may be key to enabling the whole congregation to move forward into a new normal together in unity. Our homecoming will retain familiar valued landmarks, but our perspective has widened. Worship may now include new riches and, post-Coronavirus, a virtual media element previously unimagined.

Pilgrim Routes and Memorial Churches

A so-called memorial church was built to mark the burial site of a saint or martyr. As Christian pilgrims came to visit these sites, pilgrim routes would gradually become established, sometimes linking several churches together. The Two Saints Way draws on the inspiration of St Werburgh at Chester Cathedral and St Chad (instrumental in shaping Werburgh's faith) at Lichfield. In remembering such figures, the faith of today's pilgrims can be shaped and built up through simple prayers:

> Be with us, Lord, as we seek to follow in the footsteps of your servant Chad,
> whose humility and prayerfulness attracted so many to your kingdom.
> Let our lives, like his, reflect the light of Christ and the hope of faith.
> In the name of your Son Jesus Christ, our Lord. Amen.

The Two Saints route passes by the church of martyr St Wulfad in Stone. Together with the two cathedrals, St Mary's Nantwich, Englesea Brook Primitive Methodist Chapel, Stoke Minster and St Chad's Stafford offer further opportunities to pause for short acts of worship.

Outside the church of St Wendreda, March, the vaulted passageway under the tower preserves an ancient right of way. Through the squint windows in the passageway the eye is drawn down the length of the church towards the holy table and the sacrament at the heart of worship. Specially written prayers can combine aspects of heritage in meaningful ways for present-day pilgrims.

> God of our pilgrimage,
> we thank you for the saints who have gone before us;
> we thank you for the life and witness of St Wendreda,
> for her example of godly charity and devotion
> which brought good counsel, forgiveness and healing to many.
> We remember those who walked the ancient passageway
> under the tower and looked in towards the sanctuary;

may we recognize your divine presence with us always
both inside and outside the church...[11]

At many sites we may discover special prayers, old and new. The ancient site of Bardney Abbey, Lincolnshire, was excavated in 2011 leading to the suggestion of an open-air service on St Oswald's day (5 August). This resulted in the writing of the Bardney Prayer. A collaborative approach to writing gives this prayer authenticity and ownership by the whole congregation who use it regularly. Today, the preferred version uses a responsive format:

Father, we thank you for Bardney, which through the generations
has been a place of prayer and devotion to you.
Thank you for the real and lively sense of your presence
in this place today.
Thank you for the influence that godly men and women
have had in Bardney and the surrounding area over the centuries.
Thank you for calling us to be part of today's community
of your people...

The prayer continues with thanksgiving for St Lawrence, St Oswald and St Francis, before turning to petition, praying for transformation, inspiration, witness and church growth.[12]

In 2019, during a pilgrimage day to explore stunning medieval angel roofs in four churches in East Anglia, the liturgy and prayers deliberately drew attention to significant features:

We thank God for those who have worshipped here before us,
for the faithful believers of many centuries...
...And as we look to the roof, we remember the angels and archangels
and the great company of heaven who will one day welcome us home.
For all that God has given:
Thanks be to God.[13]

Early music specialist Silas Wollston had chosen a piece of music to match the date of each angel roof, recapturing the sound and style of the period. A combination of liturgy and music propelled the pilgrims forward with a growing awareness of the numinous and our final heavenly destination, culminating with Stanford's setting of Psalm 150 under the lantern of Ely Cathedral which depicts this psalm. The angel roofs might captivate us with their architectural conception, fine carpentry and artistic use of colour but, more importantly, they remind us of the close connection between heaven and earth as we worship. We are caught up in worship together with the great company of heaven.

Pilgrimage as a Journey of Life

'Christian tradition has always regarded pilgrimage as a way of life, the believer's earthly existence seen as a continuing journey towards a heavenly goal.'[14] This well-worn image provides a different model again for an act of worship. Specially designed to accompany the 2020 Year of Pilgrimage, RSCM's *To be a Pilgrim* Community Voices Festival is structured in six sections:

I Gathering
II Setting out on the Pilgrim Way
III Journeying through the good times
IV Journeying through the hard times
V Journey's End—the heavenly destination
VI Conclusion[15]

We are all on a journey through life, so there are potential connections for everyone. Like all pilgrimages, this symbolic journey in worship could be made time after time. It will never be the same because life will have moved on and it may be made with different groups of people. This is acknowledged in the opening liturgy.

Pilgrimage is one of the most ancient and widespread of all religious activities.
Today we are invited to journey through the centuries,
giving thanks for those who have gone before us,
those who travel with us,
and those who will follow after us.
We will walk this way together
with Jesus Christ in our midst.
We journey forward in faith
with the Holy Spirit as our companion and guide.

We cannot do pilgrimage in a hurry, so creating a sense of expansive space is important to allow reflection on our journey of faith.

We walk in the footsteps of patriarchs and prophets.
We tread this way with thanksgiving,
following their example of faith.
We walk in the footsteps of the apostles and the early church.
We tread this way with joy,
following the call of Christ.
We walk in the footsteps of the saints across the centuries.
We tread this way with grace
in the knowledge that God goes with us.

Accompanied by meaningful readings, poetry and song, such a service may offer opportunity to address unresolved tensions or difficulties in our lives within a safe space. We are simply yet powerfully reminded that Christ walks with us in a pilgrim creed by Australian liturgist, Dorothy McRae-McMahon.

> **...We believe in Jesus Christ**
> **who entered our unknown journey**
> **and experienced all our living,**
> **who walked in our earthiness**
> **and can still be discovered**
> **in our midst...**[16]

We hold within ourselves a deep tension between wanting to move on from where we are and an equally strong desire to feel settled and at rest. This innate restlessness may be a powerful reminder that as Christians we are sojourners on earth ever journeying through life to a final heavenly destination.

An alternative route for a pilgrimage service as a journey of life might be a service using waymarks from *The Pilgrim's Progress.* We can follow Christian from the City of Destruction via the Slough of Despond, Vanity Fair and Delectable Mountains to the Celestial City. We can be confronted with our sinfulness by characters such as Obstinate, Shame, Ignorance, know the assurance of forgiveness as we leave our burdens at the cross, and be encouraged on further by Prudence, Faithful and Hopeful. The role of worship leader and preacher might be aligned with the Evangelist and the Interpreter.

Stations of the Cross and Other Seasonal Journeys

In many ways, these liturgies sit between the previous two types, with echoes of the actual journey through Jerusalem as well as the pathway through life. Journeying with Christ through Holy Week and Easter can be a profound experience for many Christians, as the sufferings of Jesus are brought into sharper focus. For centuries pilgrims have followed the journey to the cross, although it did not become known as the *via sacra* in Jerusalem until the Middle Ages. The re-enactment was then brought back to the local cathedral or church, gradually taking on a more sacramental flavour.

Stations of the Cross, following the route of Jesus from Pilate's house to Calvary, were interpreted in various different ways with the idea of recapturing the worship of Jerusalem back home. By the end of the seventeenth century the custom of placing stations (usually fourteen) in churches was becoming relatively common and devotions to accompany the pictures had begun to appear. Owing to increasing ecumenical interest, there have been attempts to create a wholly scriptural set with the addition of a fifteenth station depicting the resurrection.[17] For obvious reasons, these stations must be visited in the correct order. The stations are used in the context of Good Friday. However, sculptor Toddy Hoare warns of the dangers of relegating the Stations to Lent and Holy Week and encourages us to engage with them all year round, because 'We need to confront ourselves constantly with Christ's saving work.'[18]

Treated with intentionality and preparation, engagement with these stations takes on many facets of pilgrimage: expectancy; facing doubts and unbelief; silence to create an internal sacred space; ritual to externalize change within; offering, leaving behind a part of oneself or letting go in search of a better life; perseverance and commitment. As we worship, we encounter with Christ, celebrating his death and resurrection in our own lives. Then we are sent out from worship once more, acknowledging that our pilgrimage is never over.

There is always a danger that established religious imagery may limit wider imagination. *Together for a Season* includes traditional Stations in its resources for all-age worship, but takes the principle of journey and expands it further, offering a choice of pathways to guide us through other seasons, Sunday by Sunday. Pathways for Advent, Christmas and Epiphany involve the wreath, the crib and the Jesse tree. Pathways for Lent, Holy Week and Easter involve the Lenten tree, the use of 'head, hands and heart' and the Stations (extended to include Lent, Cross and Resurrection)[19]

We could become even more creative and consider a pathway linked to *posada*, the journey of Mary and Joseph to Bethlehem and their search for lodging, continued after Christmas with the contemporary resonances of their flight into Egypt as refugees and asylum seekers. Or alternatively a pathway linked to wisdom, following the journey of the Magi from the East, picking up the great Advent '*O sapientia*' (O Wisdom) antiphon, moving through to Epiphany and ideas of manifestation and revelation. Figures of Mary and Joseph or the Magi could physically move around the community, encouraging corporate engagement through short acts of worship on arrival at each home.

Questions for Reflection

- Which examples and models of pilgrimage worship do you find most appealing? Why?
- In the light of this chapter, how might you use these models to encourage personal spirituality and growth in yourself and others?
- These examples may act as a springboard. What other 'pathways' might be explored?

4 Creating a 'Worship Pilgrimage' Round a Church or Community

We have already seen that Stations of the Cross and labyrinths were used as forms of pilgrimage to bring Jerusalem to the local church for those unable to travel there. The Methodist pilgrimage initiative suggests that key principles of making a pilgrimage can apply to welcoming visitors to a local church, whether it is a new build opening for the first time or a historic one. There is a story to tell to help others encounter God today. Throughout a church building, we can identify places and objects of architectural or historical significance. Such features can provide a connection to the church of the living, not the dead.

Creating an Atmosphere of Welcome and Invitation

Many churches, particularly in rural locations, are usually open daily. Visits can be transformed from mere historical sightseeing trips into uplifting spiritual experiences through engaging worshipfully with a mapped route round features and furnishings. The same material can be readily threaded together to produce a meaningful act of worship for the regular congregation, perhaps providing a fresh approach in places where the patronal festival is celebrated. Within a context with multiple church buildings, simple acts of worship in each church can be combined with a walk to form a longer pilgrimage.

The short journey across the threshold into a church may be difficult for some people, accompanied by questions of self-worth and acceptance, or the result of unwelcoming behaviour in the past. The opportunity to explore a new pilgrim route might entice the reluctant inside. At the very least there needs to be a clear and obvious sign at the entrance porch inviting people to come inside, perhaps with a simple prayer.

Worship for a People on the Move

Unlike self-contained prayer stations, there is an inbuilt assumption that pilgrimage will take us on a journey, providing a specific route which is just as important as the places to pause. Why not intentionally use the structure of a service to map the route round the building? Where are the good places to pause to enable preparation, word, prayer, sacrament, sending? How can we create an imaginative route with changes of posture, action and involvement to enrich the worship experience whilst avoiding clumsiness or destroying atmosphere? What features of the building will readily facilitate the journey, both the familiar and the unusual? Consider thresholds, doorways and steps; statues, paintings, icons and banners; carvings, Scripture panels and stained glass; grave slabs and tombs or memorials on the wall.

Most churches will be dedicated to a patron saint, but we can also give thanks for the saints who form the regular worshipping congregation today. Our pilgrim worship can become earthed in the present by using as foci for reflection the practicalities of seating, lighting, heating, the children's area, kitchen facilities or toilets, which are all part of welcome and hospitality. Noticeboards or photo boards can introduce us to the current church family and highlight important links to local charities and overseas mission.

And what of choir stalls, organ or piano? Music may be tricky to include in an empty building, but what about using hymnody as spoken prayer? Encourage pilgrims to bring to mind hymns or songs they know and treasure, but also provide some appropriate hymn words for reflection. Brief instructions will be needed at each stopping place to aid worship and reflection, readily identified by a repeated pilgrim symbol or logo. The route can also be outlined in a pilgrim worship leaflet.

Preparation

Here is a sample prayer to be placed near the main entrance to get people started:

> God of our pilgrimage,
> open our eyes to your presence,
> open our minds to your grace,
> open our lips to your praises,
> open our lives to your healing,
> and be found among us as we journey,
> through Jesus Christ our Lord.
> Amen.

The font might be the first dominant feature at the west end and can be kept topped up with fresh water. This may provide one option for an act of confession with renewal of baptism vows, using the words of The Decision for repentance and turning to Christ followed by the signing of the cross. Alternatively, many churches still have hassocks. Pilgrims may be invited to kneel in a pew or at the communion rail with some simple words of contrition. We kneel less often in worship these days, but this conscious change of posture can be powerful.

The Word of God

Both lectern and pulpit are usually dominant features at the front of the nave. Wood carved depictions of the four gospel writers or the symbol of the eagle at the lectern remind us of the proclamation of the gospel to the world. Here we can give thanks for successive preachers, but we can also be challenged. Testimony is a corporate act. If we had the opportunity to address the congregation today, what good news would we want to communicate?

Many churches will have a large (and possibly old) lectern Bible that could act as a focus. A copy of a contemporary translation such as Eugene Peterson's *The Message* or Rob Lacey's *The Word on the Street* might be placed alongside for pilgrims to browse, bringing familiar texts to life in a new way.

Some churches, such as Moulton St Mary, Norfolk, feature wall plaques of the Ten Commandments, the Lord's Prayer and the Apostles' Creed. Together with the Beatitudes, these core texts appear in the under-used *Common Worship* 'Rites on the Way' materials for supporting disciples on the way of Christ. 'The Affirmation of the Christian Way' could be an appropriate worship text here.[20]

Prayer

The architecture and furniture can be used as a stimulus for individual prayer as we journey around the building but it can also be part of corporate prayer, prayed with eyes open and with plenty of space to reflect.

We thank God for those who have worshipped here before us,
for the faithful believers of many centuries.

At the door, we remember those who have come in
and those who have passed by.
At the font, we remember those who have been baptized
and have entered into the community of the church.
At the pulpit, we remember successive preachers
who have proclaimed the word of God.
At the holy table, we remember Christ,
our host, who feeds and sustains us on our journey.

Other specific features of the church could be added here, ending:

For all that God has given:
Thanks be to God.[21]

Alternatively, prayers could link directly with a specific feature within the church building, such as bell towers, rood screens, significant tombs or even a consistory court!

The crossing or chancel step is a threshold which might easily be passed over, and yet it is a place of life-changing significance and solemnity: commitment to marriage; commitment to a new ministry; or in a funeral, the commendation of a loved one to God's mercy and everlasting care. A pause for reflection here could be transformative.

Sacraments

At the holy table, we are welcomed by Christ and we remember the generations who have gathered around the table before us. A basket and slips of paper can be provided to name those with whom we have shared in the past. In this place of thanksgiving the words of the contemporary communion hymn, 'Behold the Lamb who bears our sins away' might provide a helpful focus and a reminder of the continuing journey until we all feast in heaven 'around the table of the King.'[22] The rich repertoire of hymns for Holy Communion may offer other suitable words for worship and reflection.

Sending

An appropriate sending is straightforward when we all worship together corporately, but it may be more difficult to draw an individual act of pilgrimage to a close in a dynamic way. It is worth considering carefully how to finish and where we might expect that to happen. How do we want to leave people and how do we want them to leave?

A Blessing
May God the Father who created you, guide your footsteps,
may God the Son who redeemed you, share your journey,
may God the Holy Spirit who sanctifies you, lead you on life's pilgrimage,
and the blessing of God, Father, Son and Holy Spirit
be with you wherever you may go.
Amen.[23]

This blessing or a prayer of commitment and protection such as St Patrick's Breastplate could be printed on small cards to take away, as pilgrims continue their life's journey.

Some Practicalities

If a pilgrimage service is used with a congregation, there are practicalities to consider, particularly in relation to the size of the building and the size of the congregation. In a cathedral or large church, it might be possible for the whole body of people to move in procession from place to place, and equally a smaller group within a small church. It is worth noting that the movement of any congregation takes time and will require clear directions to ensure smooth transition. However, movement can be impractical in a small building with a sizeable congregation. In this situation, the leader of worship can move from place to place around the building and the congregation may be encouraged to journey with their eyes to engage as fully as possible.

Short acts of worship can be replicated in different churches and combined to form a benefice, circuit or ecumenical churches together pilgrimage, stopping at other significant places within the community on the way. This might provide a fresh and uplifting approach to Rogation and walking the bounds, or it could be included within the ten days of prayer between Ascension Day and Pentecost as part of the prayer initiative, Thy Kingdom Come.[24] Pilgrimage can also be an important mission tool, reminding people of God's presence and forging a deeper connection between church and community. It can be an effective way of connecting, for instance, with local schools.

Travelling in God's Creation

Churchyards, too, have special meaning for local people. Peace and tranquillity intermingle here with a sense of sanctity. The church porch or lychgate, cultivated quiet gardens of remembrance or natural areas may provide good stopping places. Gardens are significant in Scripture, providing material for reflection. Psalms such as Psalm 24, 'The earth is the Lord's,' and Psalm 148, 'Let all creation praise the name of the Lord,' and the Benedicite, a Song of Creation, together with many hymns on the theme of creation, give voice to praise. Indeed, the churchyard may provide the perfect starting point for a pilgrimage further afield centred around creation and the care of the environment, in which participants experience the simple pleasure of reconnecting with nature and enjoying its beauty.

This type of pilgrimage is not place specific. It is flexible and adaptable, although it requires intentionality and planning. Generosity towards the earth and towards other human beings is inherent in the celebration of Rogation. Alternatively, we might make a pilgrimage in a city centre and open ourselves up to encountering God in the clash of cultures between the consumer-driven retail world and the poverty of homelessness. God is neither left at home nor only waiting at the destination but is encountered on the journey. All these different approaches open us up to new insights and possibilities to make pilgrimages in our own context.

Useful Resources

Simon Bailey, *Stations* (Sheffield: Cairns Publication, 1991) Pilgrimage round a home.

Iona Community, *A Road to Roam: A Way of Celebrating Sacred Space,* (Glasgow: Wild Goose Resource Group, 2006) Pilgrimage round a church.

Sally Welch, *Every Place is Holy Ground: Making a Pilgrimage Through Everyday Places* (Norwich: Canterbury Press, 2011) Pilgrimage round a home, church, community.

Bob Jackson, *Peak Pilgrimage* (Eyam: Mompesson Press, 2015) Combining walks and churches.

Questions for Reflection

As a worshipper:

- What strikes you when you first walk into your local church when it is empty?
- How are you made welcome and invited in?

As a worship leader:

- What features draw the eye?
- How might they be used to create a journey of worship?
- How important is a clear beginning or ending for an act of pilgrimage?

5 Hymnody and Other Resources

We now turn our attention to music for pilgrimage. Indeed, what do pilgrims sing? And do hymns need to mention pilgrims specifically in the lyrics? It is not uncommon to find people listening to worship music on portable devices, as they walk along. The same might apply to an individual walking a labyrinth. Here, it is a matter of personal choice, but what of corporate worship, when people sing together *en route* or at the end of a pilgrimage, or during a service in a local church, picking up pilgrim themes? Many suggestions could resource any or all of these, but not every song would work in each context.

Psalms of Ascent

The Psalms of Ascent (120–134), also known as Pilgrim Psalms, are some of the oldest songs for pilgrimage. Many scholars believe they were sung by those going up to Jerusalem for the great Jewish festivals.[25] This was a dangerous, arduous undertaking, so there are strong themes of dependency on God for help and protection. The majority are cheerful, and all inspire hope, encouraging worshippers as they journey together on their way to God. Again, we find the tension between journey, 'Let us go to the house of the Lord,' and destination, an emphasis on Jerusalem / Zion (Ps 122.1–4). These psalms continue to be important in their own right within pilgrim worship today, but they also introduce us to some helpful principles for worship on the move. They are all short, with formulaic phrases and repetition to aid memory.

Short Chants

Short chants are equally useful for moving people from one place to another, otherwise singing can become a bit hit and miss. Simplicity and brevity mean we do not need printed words, and we can sing unaccompanied. We only need a confident singer and perhaps a recorder or pitch pipe to get started, and when we are walking it does not matter if the song gradually peters out. South African 'We are marching' ('*Siyahamba*') (is an obvious choice, but there are many others particularly from the world church which are repetitive and easy to learn):

'Send out your light,' Iona Community

'Come with me for the journey is long' ('*Hamba Nathi*') South Africa

Other verses can be added, *eg* 'Sing/pray/dance/walk with me for the journey is long'

'We will walk with God, my brothers/sisters' ('*Sizohamba naye*') Swaziland traditional

'We walk his way' ('*Ewe, thina*') Xhosa[26]

Archbishop Sentamu played Taizé chants on his phone during his pilgrimage around the Diocese of York in 2015 and 2016. Rounds, too, may be effective. Spirituals offer another source of readily memorable material with a strong emphasis on our heavenly destination, for example: 'O when the saints go marching in,' 'Swing low, sweet chariot' and the more melancholy 'Steal away, steal away, oh Lord oh, steal away to Jesus.'

Hymns and Songs

Max Kramer, Precentor of Canterbury Cathedral, points out that processions are the liturgical expression of pilgrimage, which remains to be rediscovered despite the number of hymns in some hymnbooks explicitly marked for processional use.[27]

There are obvious hymns like 'Guide me, O thou great redeemer' with its allusions to the Israelites' journey through the wilderness and Bunyan's 'Who would true valour see' with its direct references 'to be a pilgrim' beset with various challenges. Familiar texts such as 'Through the night of doubt and sorrow' can be refreshed by using a different tune. The Welsh tune, EBENEZER, gives a different feel from the more usual MARCHING. Words have been updated, (for example in the 2013 *A&M*), replacing 'Brother clasps the hand of brother' with 'Pilgrim clasps the hand of pilgrim.' Similarly, 'Brother, sister let me serve you' now speaks of 'pilgrims on a journey.' The recent Methodist hymnbook *Singing the Faith* provides a rich and relevant resource in the 'Our journey with God' section (Nos 455–488). There is a strong sense here of journeying through life as well as physical space. Songs include the popular 'One more step along the world I go' by Sydney Carter, but also the beautiful Mexican traditional, 'When we are living, we are in the Lord.'

Folk tunes work well. The following hymns are set to KINGSFOLD:

'Earth's fragile beauties we possess,' Robert Willis—each verse ends with a reference to the 'pilgrim song'; it would work well with Stations of the Cross.

'Deep in the shadows of the past,' Brian Wren—remembers biblical journeys 'from Exodus to Pentecost' (in *Singing the Faith*)

'I know not where tomorrow's road,' Margaret Clarkson—reflects on 'my pilgrim way' through life (search Hope Publishing website)

John Bell offers enticing hymns of invitation, 'Will you come and follow me' to KELVINGROVE and 'Jesus Christ is Waiting' (last verse—'Who will join my journey') to NOEL NOUVELET.

Well-known contemporary hymnwriters offer various possibilities:

Timothy Dudley-Smith

- 'We turn to Christ anew' (LEONI)—speaks of walking and journey
- 'The pilgrim church of God' (LEONI)
- 'When the way is hard to find' (DIX, HEATHLANDS or ST PETERSBURGH)

Martin Leckebusch

- 'Pilgrims of the risen Lord' (CHARITY or ANDERSON)—travelling the pilgrim way daily 'steering to the heavenly land'
- 'Jesus we have heard your spirit' (BLAENWERN or ODE TO JOY)—a chosen pilgrim people journeying together

Andrew Pratt

- 'A scallop shell the badge of our devotion' (INTERCESSOR)—recently penned at a Hymn Society meeting with obvious links to the Camino

A different musical approach is offered by Stuart Townend, particularly through his 2011 album *The Journey*:

Vagabonds—arranged in a pacey folk style with strings and whistles

'Christ be in my waking'—gentle and reflective to accompany us in our daily walk with resonance to the Liturgy of Hours

Poetry

St Hywen's Church, Aberdaron, presents a 'Pilgrimage through the poetry of RS Thomas: Stations to the untenanted Cross.' Using the poems in *Etched by Silence*, participants are guided around the church, stopping at eight separate stations to listen to one or two poems, followed by silent reflection.[28]

Poems can be interspersed within the liturgy of a service, and might provide a good alternative to preaching. Here are a few suggestions:

His Pilgrimage, Walter Raleigh—reflecting on life and death as a pilgrimage

The Pilgrimage, George Herbert—references Bunyan's classic

The Road Not Taken, Robert Frost—taking 'the road less travelled'

Maps, Holly Ordway—connects ancient maps with today's SatNav

Art

Jonathan Clark's millennium sculpture, *The Way of Life* in Ely Cathedral depicts a winding path that travels from darkness to light, leading us to Christ. We can spot a tiny human figure on the top arm, symbolic of someone on the journey of faith. Christian artist, He Qi's *Road to Emmaus* (1997) captures movement and draws us into the journey. The vivid colours hint at the joy to come as the disciples listen to Jesus. There are many paintings of the seventeenth century Pilgrim Fathers setting out on the Mayflower or arriving in America. They identified closely with the Israelites in their exodus from slavery to freedom, but today we might make links with refugees and asylum seekers.

Multi-sensory Elements

The Israelites held their symbolic meal as part of Passover and built real booths as part of the Feast of Tabernacles, and the practices of building cairns or lighting votive candles have long histories as an act of devotion, gratitude, penitence, intercession or commitment. We readily associate the scallop shell with pilgrims returning from Santiago, but I have a growing collection of symbols from pilgrim services—a piece of slate, several olive wood crosses, a piece of broken pottery. There is something profoundly important about returning with a token as a reminder of a journey shared and experienced with God and with others.

Questions for Reflection

- Which hymns and songs stand out to you as potential pilgrim songs?
- What poetry or art might enhance worship on the way?
- What images or objects might you carry with you or retain to encourage further worship and prayer?

6 Final Thoughts

Pilgrimage is a living tradition today, ever conscious of its past but always alert to new possibilities, part of a continuous thread linking ancient traditions with contemporary culture. Worship can be integral, enriching and deepening the experience in fresh and creative ways. However, we must always be cautious how we reinterpret pilgrimage today in order to avoid a Christian romanticism which can be wistful and nostalgic, or a pick-and-mix spirituality which draws us away from Christian truth.

Both pilgrimage and worship hold together tensions:

- A focus on destination and the importance of where we are now;
- A focus on journey and the importance of the next step;
- An embracing of the small local and the large focal;
- An engagement with the spiritual and the material together;
- A growing self-awareness and an awareness of others and of God.

The compulsion and paradox of pilgrimage resonate with the complexity of human experience and our journey through life with its own tensions between a deep-seated desire to travel and an equally strong desire to feel settled. We come together to share in worship at fixed times and in specific places, but at the same time we offer worship to God sacrificially within the continuum of everyday life. The journey is never over and we are spurred ever onwards to the final heavenly city in which worship will continue without end.

This booklet is designed to whet the appetite for further journeys of discovery. Let us set out with an openness to meet with God and to be strengthened in our faith in new and unexpected ways. We go with the intention of embracing mystery and searching for a deeper connection with God, with the numinous and with others. We will worship alone and corporately, and we will discover treasures old and new as we travel. For worship leaders, the suggestions and examples can be used in their original form or they can be readily adapted to the local context. Learning to be adaptable is the mark of a real pilgrim!

Most important...

- Set out, and see where the Spirit leads.
- Be real and focus on what really matters.

- Live in and savour the present moment with thanksgiving.
- And may a song of joy rise up and our hearts sing, as we journey on.

Notes

1 See www.englishcathedrals.co.uk These include pathways commemorating Celtic saints in the Isle of Man, the *Camino Ingles* (the English Way) from Finchale Abbey to Durham Cathedral and beyond, and the *Via Francigena* from Canterbury to Rome. 2020 also marks the 1000th anniversary of St Edmundsbury; the 850th anniversary of the martyrdom of Thomas Becket; the 800th birthday of the city and cathedral of Salisbury; also the 400th anniversary of the Pilgrim Fathers setting sail in the Mayflower.

2 David Osborne, *Pilgrimage* (Grove Spirituality booklet S59) and Peter Gibbs, *Pilgrimage Today* (Grove Spirituality booklet S143).

3 David Osborne, *Pilgrimage, op cit*, p 3.

4 See A McGowan, P F Bradshaw, *The Pilgrimage of Egeria: A New Translation of the Itinerarium Egeriae with Introduction and Commentary,* Alcuin Club Collections 93 (Collegeville, MN: Liturgical Press Academic, 2018). This explores what constituted pilgrimage, the origins of Christian practice and worship in holy places in detail.

5 From an address at the cathedral in Santiago de Compostela, 6 November 2010 © 2010 Libreria Editrice Vaticana, Benedict XVI>Speeches>2010>November.

6 See C O Buchanan, *Historical Dictionary of Anglicanism* (Lanham, MD: Rowman and Littlefield, second ed, 2015). A commemoration is held annually in June to remember murdered missionary, Bernard Mizeki (d 1896). Thousands of Anglican worshippers journey from all over Zimbabwe to be present. In Uganda, the murder of Archbishop Janani Luwum by Amin in 1977, together with that of Bishop Hannington and his followers in 1885/1886, is marked in a similar way with a large annual pilgrimage to the place of their martyrdom, Namugongo.

7 I Tarrant and S Dakin, *Labyrinths and Prayer Stations* (Grove Worship booklet W180) p 6.

8 R Ferguson, *George MacLeod: Founder of the Iona Community* (Glasgow: Wild Goose Publications, rev ed, 2001) p 156.

9 See A M Allchin and Esther de Waal, *Threshold of Light* (London: Darton, Longman and Todd, 1986) p 56.

10 Adapted from Kathy Galloway (ed), *The Pattern of our Days* (Glasgow: Wild Goose Publications, 1996) p 28.

11 Prayer written specially for RSCM Angel Tour Pilgrimage by Helen Bent, August 2019.

12 See 'The Bardney Prayer,' *Vibe* Issue 13, Autumn 2019, published by Rural Ministries UK.

13 See note 10.

14 J G Davies (ed), *A New Dictionary of Liturgy and Worship* (London: SCM Press Ltd, 1986) p 433.

15 *To be a Pilgrim: RSCM Community Voices Festival* (Salisbury: RSCM Press, 2021).

16 Extract from Creed, Dorothy McRae-McMahon, *Liturgies for the Journey of Life* (London: SPCK, 2000) p 127.

17 See *Common Worship Times and Seasons* (London: Church House Publishing, 2006) Stations of the Cross, p 238; also Stations of the Resurrection, using resurrection appearances of Jesus to different people, p 446.

18 Toddy Hoare, *The Stations of the Cross* (Grove Spirituality booklet S101).

19 *Together for a Season* is published in three companion volumes covering the church year (London: Church House Publishing, 2006, 2007, 2009 respectively).

20 See *Common Worship: Christian Initiation* (London: Church House Publishing, 2006) Rites on the Way, p 36.

21 Prayer at All Saints Church, Necton. See note 10.

22 Keith and Kristyn Getty and Stuart Townend. Words available at https://www.stuarttownend.co.uk/song/communion-hymn/

23 Jenny Child, from 'Pilgrims' Way,' Canterbury.

24 Thy Kingdom Come is a prayer initiative led by the Church of England. Since it began in May 2016, it has grown into a global and ecumenical prayer movement to further the witness and mission of the Christian church. Discover more at www.thykingdomcome.global

25 See T Dowley, *Christian Music: A Global History* (Oxford: Lion Hudson, 2011) p 23.

26 The Iona Community publishes many possibilities in their pocket-sized 'wee song' books, but some chants also appear in recent hymnbooks. An extended list of hymns and songs with their sources is offered as an online resource to support this booklet.

27 See the article 'Becket2020 at Canterbury Cathedral: The Way of Worship,' Max Kramer, in *Praxis News of Worship* Issue 64, December 2019.

28 A collection compiled and published by Jim Cotter, retired vicar of St Hywyn's, Aberdaron, specifically for the modern-day pilgrim. Selected for their accessibility and connection with the church, Ynys Enlli and seascape of Aberdaron.